Vassar: A Photographic Celebration

A Photographic Celebration
Vassar

MARK C. BORTON

EMBASSY IMPRINT, INC. / HADDAM / CONNECTICUT

Library of Congress Card Catalog No. 84-081553

ISBN 0-930527-00-3 (softcover)
ISBN 0-930527-01-1 (hardcover)
ISBN 0-930527-02-X (special edition)

Manufactured in the United States of America

Dedication

We dedicate this celebration of Vassar College's beautiful campus and eventful history to the memory and spirit of Matthew Vassar's magnificent enterprise and to the continuing tradition of excellence he established.

Matthew Vassar, Founder

Introduction

MATTHEW VASSAR had no heirs. Yet today, 30,000 women and men have good reason to celebrate his wisdom, foresight, and generosity.

Vassar was a poor immigrant turned self-made millionaire who wished to do something for the betterment of society. At the suggestion of Milo Jewett, a local minister and educator, Vassar founded and endowed the first women's college in the world. His college was to be the equal of the finest institutions for men—a college in the grand style, with well-stocked libraries, extensive art galleries, the most up-to-date scientific equipment, and a distinguished faculty. Creating such a college was an ambitious project for a man who was himself without a college education. But Vassar's single-minded determination proved equal to the task. The college has flourished ever since on the principles and traditions he established.

Symbolizing Vassar's revolutionary idea, and the grandness of his enterprise, stood Main Building. It was as large as it was unusual—housing the President's apartment, professors' rooms, students' rooms, classrooms, laboratories, and even the laundry room—all under one roof. But Matthew Vassar endowed his college with more than a building. He gave the college a sense of community and an unswerving commitment to excellence.

One could easily photograph all of Main Building and all the buildings that have been built since without ever giving a sense of the unique spirit of the college. The photographs in this book were not taken to catalog Vassar's architecture or topography but to capture the spirit of the college. That spirit stems from individual devotion to excellence and a desire to achieve—secured by shared experience and a sense of community. Each additional building has been a physical manifestation of that spirit, as each new generation has contributed to the growth of the college. And for each succeeding generation the evolving campus itself has been a source of insight, understanding, and inspiration.

To photograph the moments when the beauty of the campus today is most inspirational, we took almost 5,000 pictures. We captured the autumn shadows as they stretched across the buildings and trees. We woke early on winter mornings to photograph virgin snow in the Quad. And we sprinted around the lake to catch the thousand yellows and greens of the daffodil fields before the next cloudburst.

But capturing a sense of the beauty of Vassar today was not enough. We also wanted to show how the spirit of the college came to be what it is. In the Rare Book Room of the Library we found original material photographed and penned by the students, faculty, and administrators who have helped shape Vassar College. From among tens of thousands of photographs in the college collection we have selected 50 of the most interesting and evocative to include in our *Celebration*. We have also selected and reprinted personal letters and other documents (complete with original spellings and punctuation) to give a sense of the intimate feelings that people have held for Vassar throughout the last century and a quarter.

We hope that this book is a tangible representation of the indomitable spirit of Vassar College. And we hope that you, too, will be inspired by Matthew Vassar's dream—a dream of creating the finest institution of learning in the world.

Mark C. Borton '84

A History of Vassar College

VASSAR COLLEGE, founded in 1861 by Matthew Vassar, a successful English-born brewer and businessman, has a long and unique history as an educational institution with distinctive traditions. Matthew Vassar's purpose was to offer women a liberal arts education equal to that of the best men's colleges of the day. He established his college in Poughkeepsie, a small city on the Hudson River, 75 miles north of New York City, and now the center of the Mid-Hudson region. The college was to be a pioneer in women's education and in liberal arts education itself.

In 1865, four years after the original charter, Vassar's great Main Building was completed, and the college opened with 353 students. Vassar's first students were by definition pioneers. At a time, right after the Civil War, when most higher education for women was thin and unambitious, young women were sent far from home—from all over the United States—to Poughkeepsie, New York, to obtain education of the same high quality that Harvard and Yale offered young men.

From the outset, Vassar was designed for the bright, the talented, the energetic, and the courageous.

Vassar College had a strong sense of its own individuality from the beginning. It was decidedly different from other institutions— the usual women's academies and seminaries of the mid-nineteenth century and the conventional men's colleges—and it viewed the world from new perspectives. Although it was not pressed with the necessity felt by many men's colleges to train clergy and lawyers, its early graduates were among the first women professionals in other fields. Vassar was free to devote itself with unusual intensity and singleness of purpose to nurturing in its students certain lifelong habits of mind and timeless values: respect for human dignity and freedom, concern for society as well as for oneself, faith in reason, and commitment to action.

Vassar has been widely known for its uncompromising insistence on the highest intellectual standards, an attitude which has its roots in the college's early

history. Since there was no women's college of the highest caliber in America in 1861, it was imperative for Vassar to prove to the world that it could, indeed, be such an institution. At that time, students were often ill-prepared for rigorous college-level work. By setting up its own preparatory department and by using its influence on girls schools, within ten years Vassar was able to set its entrance standards at the same level as colleges for men. That preparatory department was eventually abolished and the institution's collegiate standards became fully established.

Education at Matthew Vassar's college was shaped by faculty members distinguished both for scholarly achievement and dedication to undergraduate teaching. Among those early faculty members were the noted astronomer Maria Mitchell, the first woman to be elected to the American Academy of Arts and Sciences, and Frederick Louis Ritter, one of America's first music historians. From the beginning, instruction was vigorous and imaginative. In 1869,

Miss Mitchell took her students to Iowa to observe an eclipse of the sun; in the 1880s, Lucy Maynard Salmon was teaching history from original sources by the seminar method. Intellectual rigor of this kind led to the founding at Vassar in 1898 of the first chapter of Phi Beta Kappa at a women's college.

By 1915, the college had grown to 1,000 students, the curriculum had moved toward the elective system, and most of the modern academic departments had been created. In 1919, Vassar, with Smith, Wellesley, and Mount Holyoke, adopted a plan of admission using a competitive examination developed by the newly formed College Entrance Examination Board. During the 1920s, the curriculum became deeper, broader, and more varied. The faculty was larger and more distinguished; and the social consciousness and the sense of social responsibility that are characteristic of the Vassar community were becoming visible to the world. Students and alumnae paraded for causes, organized meetings and committees, raised money, and devoted themselves to the issues of the day. Indeed, during the '20s and '30s, the "Vassar girl" was sometimes a popular exemplar of movements for social change.

A particularly significant example of institutional change was the trustees' adoption, in 1923, of the Vassar College Statute of Instruction, later known as the Governance, which provided for a high degree of faculty participation in educational decision making. This full faculty participation—at issue at most institutions—has shaped all of Vassar's subsequent history. This same period saw the evolution of revised and expanded powers of the student association. Student government was concerned primarily with the organization of student life.

During World War II, Vassar experimented with a three-year program. After the war, Vassar's first men students appeared, as about 100 veterans took courses between 1946 and 1950. During the 1950s, enrollment grew to 1,500, and new buildings were constructed. With the aid of the Mary Conover Mellon Fund for the Advancement of Education, student counseling services were extended and improved, and Vassar pioneered in basic research into psychological change during the college years—research that proved of value not only to Vassar but to other institutions as well.

As the college celebrated its centennial in 1961, Matthew Vassar's aims had been well realized and the name of Vassar had become a byword for excellence in women's education. More than one-quarter of the graduates held advanced degrees, and hundreds had distinguished themselves in literature, the sciences, medicine, law, teaching, journalism, the social sciences, and government; characteristically, they had been activists, organizers, movers and shakers.

For many months in 1966 and 1967, the college engaged in an intensive self-examination to determine the new dimensions it would need if it was to be as effective in the future as it had been in the past. One result of that study (Vassar's most dramatic development in the eyes of the public) was coeducation. True to its pioneering spirit, Vassar was the first of the long-established and prestigious women's colleges to admit men. Also as a result of the study, Vassar reconstructed its curriculum, embarked on a major building program, increased its enrollment to 2,250, and enlarged the faculty. Social regulations for students were liberalized, and students acquired more opportunities for self-government and a greater share in the processes by which college decisions are made. There was a renewed and more active interest among many students and faculty members in relating the concerns of the college to the concerns of the larger community and the world beyond the college.

To acquire the financial resources needed for change and growth, the college carried on a Capital Campaign, completed at the end of 1973, which raised $52 million in gifts and pledges for academic programs and for buildings.

All those changes were made in a spirit inherited from Vassar's past: a determination to excel, a willingness to experiment, a dedication to the values of the liberal arts and sciences, a commitment to the advancement of equality between the sexes, and the development of leadership. That spirit remains paramount at Vassar as the college consolidates the gains of its era of expansion.

Major fund-raising campaigns were begun during the '80s. These funds will enable the college to strengthen the academic program as well as to expand the academic and athletic facilities, ensuring that Vassar's standards of excellence will be maintained in the future.

Presidents of Vassar College

Milo P. Jewett	1861-1864
John H. Raymond	1864-1878
Samuel L. Caldwell	1878-1885
James Monroe Taylor	1886-1914
Henry Noble MacCracken	1915-1946
Sarah Gibson Blanding	1946-1964
Alan Simpson	1964-1977
Virginia B. Smith	1977-

Adapted from the Vassar College Catalogue 1984-85.

Taylor Gate

The Porter's Lodge

October 22d 1897

. . . The walk to the Porter's Lodge and the Lodge itself is unchanged. I remember walking down there in the rain one day in hopes of catching a glimpse of Miss [Louisa May] Alcott who was expected to arrive that day. She had come by a morning train, so all we saw was a small battered, canvas-covered trunk marked "A"—which an express man was bringing up from the city and which we girls looked at with loving admiration so great was our affection for the gifted owner.

Letter from Kate Berry Morey to her daughter, Jeanette Morey

I hope you will get three things
out of college: a sense of
discovery, a sense of style, and
a point of view of your own.

Alan Simpson
(President, Vassar College, 1964-1977)

Main Building

Main Building

Main Building (Stereoscopic View)

Main Building

Main Building

The College edifice will attract attention. It was designed by J. Renwick, Jun., of the firm of Renwick, Auchmuty, & Sands, from plans furnished by Professor Milo P. Jewett, now the President of the College. The building is to be of brick, four stories high, with capacity to accommodate 300 students, each having her own separate sleeping-room. It will contain a Chapel, Library, Art Gallery, Lecture and Recitation rooms, etc. It will be abundantly supplied with pure, soft water, lighted with gas, and heated by steam. It will be nearly fire-proof. The location is about a mile and a half east of the city of Poughkeepsie, on grounds embracing two hundred acres in extent.

From "Vassar Female College"
in Harper's Weekly, *March 30, 1861*

Main Building

Repeated requests on the part of Sarah J. Hale, editor of *Godey's Lady's Magazine,* prompted the elimination of the ignoble "Female" from the title "Vassar Female College." The marble tablet bearing the word "Female" was removed from the facade of Main Building prior to the College's opening in 1865.

Main Building

...Francis R. Allen designed the Soap Palace and Frederick Ferris Thompson financed it. The Palace originally served as the Vassar library. Before the Soap Palace's erection, the Vassar Library first used the third floor of Main and later the second floor of the building. The addition to Main acquired its name "Soap Palace" because its veined marble looked like a commercial soap. Students also affectionately called it "Uncle Fred's Nose," since Mr. Thompson's gift made its construction possible.

From Vassar Miscellany News
March 2, 1960

Main Building, Thompson Annex, 1958

No better symbol for a college
than a tree! Matthew Vassar must
have thought of this when he
planted his trees and when he said
that a college must be a living
entity, having capacities of growth
and of adaptability. And when
a college, like a tree, is planted by
the river of the water of life,
whatever it doeth shall prosper.

Henry Noble MacCracken
(President, Vassar College, 1915-1946)

17

October 22d 1897

...In the dining room I see no change at all. Same tables, same dishes, same enormous knives & forks, same celery glasses in the middle of the table & I believe the same celery. I think this room has enjoyed a Rip van Winkle sleep. —If anything could sleep with 300 noisy girls about. I would like to come back and taste the griddle cakes again. I never had better anywhere & it used to be fun to watch the women bake them—the few times we were allowed in the kitchen. Do they still have lady fingers & ice cream for dessert occasionally—In the Spring vacation they gave them to us every day.

*Letter from Kate Berry Morey
to daughter, Jeanette Morey*

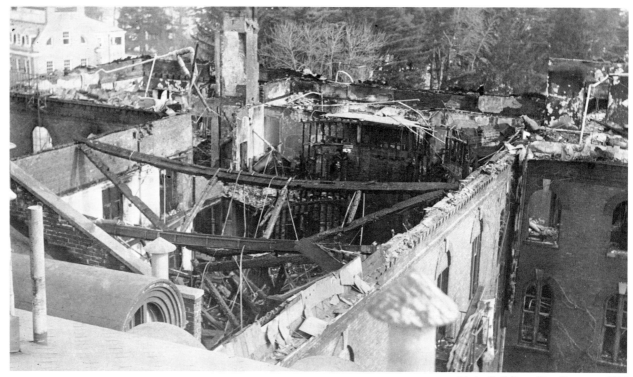

Main Building, Fire Damage, 1918

Main Building, Dining Room, ca. 1889

[*February 13, 1918*]

Well, Mother,

...I sent one [telegram] last night because I thought it might be in the papers and you know how they exaggerate. It was a bad fire, about $300,000 loss. One whole wing is gone. It started last night about half past five, and they reported a peculiar smell but as they were cooking steaks, it wasn't investigated. It was a defective flue. While the girls were at dinner, about six or a little after, the fire bell rang and every one got out of the building immediately. ... About nine they got the fire in control and I wish you could have seen the men working. I watched two men walk along inside the burning rooms and break the windows to get the draft away from the rest of the building. They climbed back and it wasn't 5 seconds later that the floor fell in! The girls stood in lines & handed things along from Main to Rocky and got a good deal out.... There was no panic through it all and quite a lot of organization. In Davison we got to bed pretty early but heard parts of Main crashing down all through the night.

From Dorothy Prentiss Schmitt

Main Building, Fire Damage, 1918

Main (

President's House

Chapel

Chapel

Chapel

Night Owls Performance in Chapel

Chapel

November 24 1866

...The time is so divided up into periods here that I find little time to do anything but prepare my lessons, though I have but three, there are so many extra duties to be performed, we are obliged to exercise just so much every day, and we have Chapel twice a day, and about two or three lectures every week. Wednesday evening we have a lecture on health from Miss [Alida] Avery, who is the resident physician here. And Saturday morning we have a talk from Miss [Hannah] Lyman on etiquet, and twice in the week we have Bible lesson. And then we have gymnastics every day.... Now when you think of all of these and great many other little things, that I cannot stop to mention, do you wonder that my time is all occupied.

Letter from "Mary" to friend, "Katie"

Chapel

Chapel

Frederick Ferris Thompson
Memorial Library

Thompson Library and Rockefeller Hall

Thompson Library

Leaded windows throughout the main section of Thompson Library represent 15th- and 16th-century printers' symbols.
The designs are made from the printer's initials woven into intricate trademarks.
This particular mark is that of Caligula de Bacileriis, 1503.

Thompson Library

Thompson Library

The Library and Chicago Hall

Helen D. Lockwood Library

Elena Lucrezia Cornaro Piscopia received her doctoral degree from the University of Padua in 1678—the first woman ever to receive a doctorate. The great stained-glass window in the Library depicts her in all her baroque glory as she defends her thesis. Paduan professors stand ready to bestow upon her the scholar's ermine cape and the poet's laurel wreath.

"Farmerettes" on Library Lawn, 1917

Vassar Farm, 1917

World War I drained the farmers from the fields, creating a food shortage. When, in 1917, the Government called for more farm produce, Vassar students were quick to respond. Out of a large number of applicants, twelve women were chosen to work throughout the summer on the College's 740-acre farm. Rising at 4:15 in the morning, Vassar's farmers hoed and cultivated corn, beans, and potatoes. They laid a strawberry bed of 2000 plants, raked and pitched hay, and kept the gardens weed-free. Each summer farmer met the one-time requirement of milking the cows. Each student earned 17½ cents an hour and paid $5.50 per week for a room and meals in Main.

Rockefeller Hall

Rockefeller Hall

Rockefeller Hall

Chicago Hall

Chicago Hall

Davison House

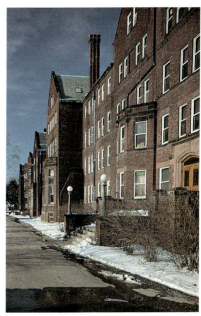

Raymond House

Raymond House

There is something contagious about Founder's Day. The most studiously blasé and the most earnestly studious find that the enthusiasm with which the rest of the college prepares for rain or shine cannot be resisted, when the day finally arrives. We gambol across the lawns or paddle over to Students'; the hot dogs and the ice-cream sandwiches disappear by hundreds; the annual faculty-student baseball game rouses more honest antagonism in our hearts than any amount of hard marking; the annual faculty play fills us with admiraion for the versatile faculty mind.

Vassarion, *1941*

Founder's Day

President MacCracken, Founder's Day, 1929

Sunday Evening 1866
May 1

My dear Madam

Words are impotent to express my feelings at the doings at your College to honor my Birth-day yesterday—to say that I was highly pleased would be a meagre reply—In truth I now learn that the heart finds things which the power of language *cannot* express, and those things occured yesterday—Please to accept my thanks for your kindness—
The scene of which will never, no never, be obliterated from my Memory.

> I remain Dear Miss G.
> Yours truly &c. &c.
> Matthew Vassar

Founder's Day, 1913

Earliest Josselyn residents were immensely envied, for they enjoyed a luxury that only their dormitory offered. The bathrooms of every floor were fitted with showers.

Josselyn House

Josselyn House

...Descending a few steps, we find ourselves in that marvelous living-room. It is decorated in dark brown mission and the walls are gold. The rugs—some really lovely oriental ones—and the massive davenports, upholstered in tapestry and a sort of maroon plush, into which one sinks luxuriously, harmonize perfectly with the room....the crowning glory of the whole room, one might say, is a magnificent Steinway Baby Grand piano standing in one corner.

From Vassar Alumnae Magazine
November 1912

On Armistice Day in 1920, a tank
was presented to Vassar by the
French government "in
recognition of the moral and
physical service" rendered by over
two hundred Vassar graduates in
France during World War I.
The so-called "Vassar Unit"—
organized in 1918 under the Red
Cross—directed eight base
hospitals. In her dedication
address, M. De Sanchez,
representing the French
government, said the French chose
this particular gift for a women's
college because the tank was
manufactured "in a factory where
over 90% of the workers were
women, whereas the 75 millimeter
gun on it was made wholly by
women." The largest war relic in
America remained in front of
Josselyn until the summer of 1934,
when it was dismantled. During the
removal, workmen found in the
tank an unexploded fuse cap and a
considerable amount of benzene.

French Tank Dedication, 1920

French Tank, Josselyn Lawn, 1921

Josselyn House and Jewett House

Jewett House and Students' Building

Jewett House

Lathrop House

Quadrangle

Quadrangle

Quadrangle, 1936

415 Raymond
Nov. 15, 1908

Dearest Folks:

If you could *see* the sight from my window this morning! The whole world is covered with a layer of snow that hides everything ugly, and the big evergreens are just loaded down, & the sun is shining so everything just sparkles. It started snowing about six o'clock yesterday—it had been gray all day—and must have snowed a good part of the night, for the fall is three or four inches thick.

From Marjorie N. MacCoy,
Class of 1911

Rockefelle

Strong House

Jewett House
and Students' Building

55

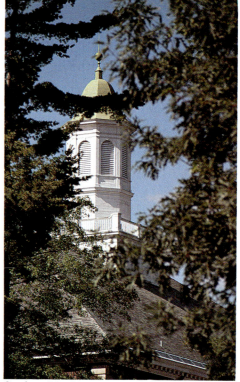

Students' Building

Students' Building

Students' Building, built in 1913 and once the center for countless concerts, dances, and dramatic presentations, became the All Campus Dining Center (ACDC) in 1973. The new, more efficient arrangement replaced the crowded and costly dining rooms in the individual dormitories.

Students' Building

Students' Building

Education is not complete unless
all powers work together.
Brain gymnastics are no more
commendable than bodily
gymnastics as mere exercise and if
one-sided are as fatal
to all-round development.

*From "Blodgett Hall of Euthenics
at Vassar College"*

Noyes Circle, ca. 1889

Winter Weekend Bonfire, 1984, Noyes Circle

Noyes House

Noyes Ho

Suffrage Parade, New York City

Student Suffrage Parade on Campus, 1912

By nature and training I am an educationist. I find the privilege of the vote has been an educational factor in my own life. In a profession which has required more than almost any other the withdrawal out of the world into the quiet library or study, my right to use the ballot has been almost the one motive which has drawn me out into real citizenship. In my capacity as teacher of men at Yale University and of women at Smith College, I have found from the point of view of education no essential difference in their grasp and mastery of intellectual problems. Any educational advantages, therefore, which belong to the one sex should, so far as I am concerned, belong properly also to the other; and since I have found the vote an educational factor in my own life I sincerely desire that it may soon be extended to women.

Henry Noble MacCracken
The Miscellany Monthly, *March 1917*

Cushing House, named in honor of Florence M. Cushing, Class of 1874, the first alumnae trustee, was built in response to concerns about dormitory overcrowding. In 1926, the Board of Trustees moved swiftly to build the new hall, "in the faith that the friends of the College, feeling that the Trustees acted rightly in building quickly, will now by their contributions help the College to meet this emergency...."

Cushing House

Cushing House

Cushing House Dining Room

65

Blodgett Hall

Blodgett Hall

Blodgett Hall

...As it happens, Vassar has long had an interest in this subject of Family Life. Ellen Swallow Richards of the Class of 1870, who was the first to coin the word "Euthenics," was a pioneer in the study of Family Life as well as the founder of the Home Economics movement. She defined Euthenics as "The betterment of living conditions, through conscious endeavor for the purpose of securing more efficient human beings."

From "Dedication of Blodgett Hall" by Minnie Cumnock Blodgett

Kenyon Hall

. . . Of course, every Vassar building must grow into its own landscape, and Kenyon Hall is not to be judged aesthetically until all its furniture has clothed it within, and the pines and birches have clothed it without; but I, for one, rest content and await the verdict of the future that the alumnae in giving Kenyon Hall to their College have again made a most signal contribution to the efficient life of their alma mater.

Henry Noble MacCracken
(President, Vassar College, 1915-1946)

Measuring 75 by 40 feet, the swimming pool in Kenyon was one of the largest indoor pools in the country.

Kenyon Hall

Helen Kenyon Hall of Physical
Education was named for
Helen Kenyon, Class of 1905, the
first woman to serve as president
of the Board of Trustees.

Wimpfheimer Nursery School

Observatory

Vassar College
Oct. 15th 1865

My Dear Mother and Father,

...I had noticed the schuttles on the dome of the observatory open for several days and wondered what observations they had been taking so I asked him [William Mitchell] and he said they had been finding their geographical position. Miss [Maria] Mitchell also said they had been studying Venus. I should like very much to take Astronomy but do not be disappointed Mother when I say I do not think I shall. It would take a great deal of time if I should, more I think than I should be willing to give to it if I am to be here only one year for I should have to go through quite a course of Mathematics before I could take Astronomy *proper* and I do not think I should care for Mathematical Astronomy much any way. I guess I have about as good an idea of Astronomy as most girls.

Ever your loving daughter
"Ellen"

Observatory

Observatory

Observatory

8.38 8.43 8.48

9.08 9.11 9.11¾

9.15 9.20 9.25

9.49 9.56 10.03

10.28

ECLIPSE of SUN
JANUARY 24 1925
AT VASSAR COLLEGE
POUGHKEEPSIE, N.Y.
PHOTOS BY C.B BORLAND.
COPYRIGHT 1925 C.B.BORLAND.

Astronomy Students, 1925

Ely Hall

Ely Hall (Alumnae Gymnasium)

Ely Hall, Faculty Aula, 1937

Ely Hall

The Alumnae Gymnasium, completed in 1889, housed dressing rooms, lockers, a large gymnastic hall, tennis courts, and a novel feature, a swimming tank, in the basement. In 1933, when a new gymnasium was built, the name of the building was changed to Ely Hall. The former basketball court became the faculty Aula—a place to hold faculty meetings and receptions. For some time, the back rooms of Ely served as an out-patient clinic with doctors' offices and nurses' quarters. Ely Hall also houses the departments of Geography and Geology, and the Museum of Natural History.

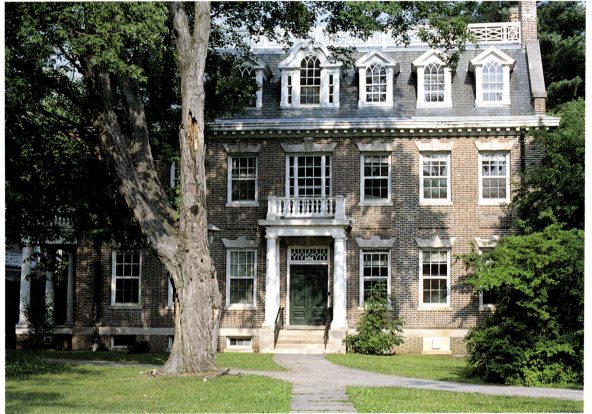

Swift Hall

...I should like you to know that many of my pleasantest college recollections cluster around our morning history class, that none of my work has been of greater help in preparation for my life as a teacher, and that I am deeply grateful to you for the inspiration which you gave to me along with the knowledge of my country's history.

Letter from Gertrude L. Chesley
to Lucy Maynard Salmon
(Professor of History, 1887-1927)

Swift Infirmary

Swift Hall, completed in 1899 and named in honor of Charles W. Swift, a charter trustee, served as the college infirmary for nearly forty years. In 1941, chairs and desks replaced charts and beds and the building became the Swift Hall of History.

Computer Center

The old Laundry Building was remodeled in 1967 to create the Vassar Computer Center. Further renovations in 1982 expanded the facilities to accommodate growing student demand for the technology.

Laundry Building

Laundry Building, 1966

...Clothes for the wash are to be sent over in a little car, running on a tramway. They will be thrown down a chute to the first floor, and pass through one of the two Smith's eccentric cylinders with which the room is furnished. In this they are to be revolved for twenty or thirty minutes. In the same apartment are stationary tubs for rinsing, bluing, and starching, a wringer, and sliding bars for drying.

From The Vassar Miscellany
November 1872

Walker Field House

Walker Field House

Terrace Apartments (Student Residences)

Sunset Lake

Sunset Hill

Vassar College
June 1, 1889

...Exams are on next week. Today Mil and I were studying Latin on Sunset Hill when Prexy [James Monroe Taylor] came along, we did not conceal our books, we talked to him as boldly as if we were not transgressing the Fourth Commandment.

> I really must stop now—
> with much love
> Nellie Furness

Letter from Caroline Furness
to sister, Mary

83

An integral part of Commencement activities, the Daisy Chain tradition dates from the late 1880's when members of the sophomore class decorated the Chapel for Commencement with daisies gathered from the College fields. Later, the decorations took the form of a rope to mark the reserved seats for seniors. Sophomores in the Class of 1894 were the first to carry the daisies as a chain. Thereafter, seniors selected a group of students from their "sister" sophomore class to carry the "two hundred feet of daisies."

Daisy Picking, 1953

Daisy Chain

Daisy Chain and Ushers

Students scoured nearby fields and neighboring estates to obtain the daisies. Assisted by professional florists, they wove the daisies into a chain. To keep the chain fresh it was floated in the gymnasium pool until Commencement.

Substituting mountain laurel for a portion of the daisies reduced the 60- to 100-pound load resting upon each sophomore shoulder to a more manageable 20 pounds.

Since 1956 the scarcity of daisies in Dutchess County has necessitated the shipment of flowers from California. The tradition of the Daisy Chain has been foregone only a few times, and then only during wartime. Men first joined the Daisy Chain as ushers with the graduating class of 1971.

...We cannot say "good-bye" to the College. Its training, its influence have become a part of us, and, if we would, we could not loosen the ties which bind us to it. And so we wish to express our very great gratitude to our Faculty who have so wisely directed this training, for helping us in ways that we will come to appreciate more and more as we grow older.

From Vassar Class Day 1906

Daisy Picking, 1912

Commencement, Outdoor Theater

Avery Hall

Avery Hall, ca. 1870

One of the earliest additions to the original campus was the Riding Academy. However, the venture was not a financial success and was closed in 1872 despite student dissent. Three years later the building was reopened as the Natural History Museum, the Art Gallery, and Studio. The Riding Academy was renovated once again in later years to produce the 400-seat Avery Theater, classrooms, and offices housing the departments of Drama, English, and Classics.

Avery Hall

Experimental Theater, 1950

Avery Hall

...There is a popular fallacy to the effect that courses in playwriting and play production bear little or no relation to the work of other college departments; and, in fact, that work in the field of the theatre is so intensive as to require concentration to the neglect of other courses. In a course properly oriented in the curriculum, the reverse should be true. The student should be made to realize that in taking up a study of the theatre he can afford to ignore nothing. He must know history in order to be at one with the full sweep of the stage from the Greeks to the moderns; he must know science, especially physics, mathematics, engineering, for the stage is no longer a painted fake, but a stage painted with light, dynamic with machines; he must know languages, for drama is of no one country, of no one language; he must know psychology, the psychology of the character he enacts, of the actors with whom he plays, of the audience which is so truly a part of the play; he must know all he can find out about sculpture, music, paintings, the dance, because the theatre synthesizes all these elements; he must know our own political, industrial, and social scene, because out of this scene the dramas of our own period are to be born.

*Hallie Flanagan Davis,
(Director of the Experimental Theatre,
1929-1945)*

Avery Hall

Ferry House

Ferry Cooperative House (Student Residences)

Seeley G. Mudd Chemistry Building

Vassar Brothers Laboratory, 1921

November 1st 1866

I am having a delightful course in Chemistry with Prof. [Charles] Farrar, who is one of the best men I ever saw. I have Eng. Literature too, and in that we have a very fine teacher. You can't imagine how nice it would be, if you were only here with me. You could take Music, German, and Painting, and you would have good teachers in them, I assure you. There are a great many here older than you, who are taking such courses. Wouldn't it be delightful? I know you would enjoy a year here very much.

Letter from Mary Pope Soper to friend, "Lina"

Ground Breaking, Sanders Physics Laboratory

Sanders Physics Laboratory

Sanders Physics Laboratory

The noble yet jovial figure of Benjamin Franklin greets students as they enter Sanders Laboratory of Physics. Cast in 1932, the elder statesman stood in a niche over the main entrance of the Harper Brothers Building in New York, surveying the promising talent of the time. When Harpers moved uptown with the rest of the publishing world, its new quarters had no place for the pewter statue.

It occurred to Burges Johnson, Professor of English at Vassar and part-time editor for Harpers, that the Vassar campus might find a suitable place for the homeless inventor. An agreement was struck, and the Benjamin Franklin statue was delivered by truck to Johnson's office.

When Johnson left Vassar in 1942, the statue remained. As his daughter later wrote, "When Father left, Benjamin was left at Vassar in the belief that probably there was no place in the country where he would feel more at home than on the campus of a female college."

A gift of alumnae living in the New England area funded the construction of New England Building. Completed in December 1901, the building originally housed the departments of Biology, Physiology, Geology, and Mineralogy. Florence M. Cushing, Class of 1874, is credited for the piece of Plymouth Rock adorning the entrance of the building. Learning that an accident had split off a portion of the rock, she traveled to Plymouth from her home in Boston and acquired the fragment for Vassar.

New England Building

96

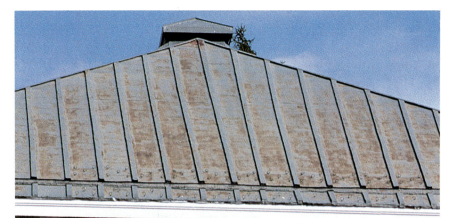

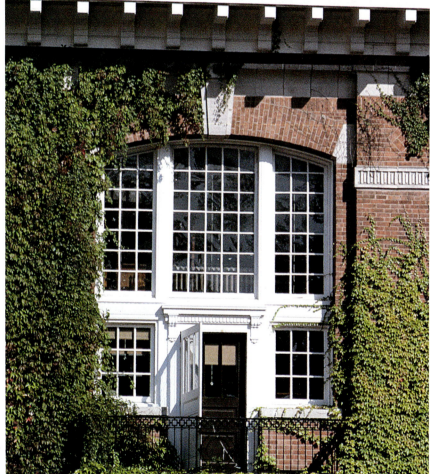

Sanders Chemistry Laboratory

...if the study of physics and chemistry is to show its peculiar excellencies alongside of the study of mathematics, of literature and of philosophy, it must be pursued in the right way. It must furnish a kind of exercise which they do not, and this is possible only when it is permitted to carry the mind of the student into actual contact with material objects and physical laws....The study of science should be the study of nature, and it is impossible to make it such without the aid of a working laboratory. The laboratory, therefore, is as indispensable to the regular college course as it is to the purely scientific and technical courses of study.

*LeRoy Cooley
(Faculty, departments of Physics and Chemistry, 1874-1907)*

Sanders Chemistry Laboratory

Olmstead Hall of the Biological Sciences

Olmstead

Olmstead

Belle Skinner Hall
of Music

...It seems most fitting that medieval Gothic of the French school should be chosen for the hall of music that is to bear Belle Skinner's name. Flanking as it does the medieval chapel, which is Norman in general character, the French Gothic of Belle Skinner Hall will balance the English Gothic of Taylor Hall on the north side of the building. As a companion building to Taylor Hall, Belle Skinner Hall is also most appropriate, for it was President [James Monroe] Taylor who began very early in his administration to desire and to ask for a special building for the Department of Music. Dean [Ella] McCaleb recalls that he wrote that it was not to be regarded "as the fancy of an ambitious college president but a necessary condition for doing the best work."

From "Belle Skinner, Vassar 1887" by Henry Noble MacCracken

Skinner

100

Vassar College Choir, Skinner Hall

Skinner

Georgia Kendrick House (Faculty Residences)

... What does it profit her if she manages to scrape through and get a degree, and yet has no comprehension of what a college like this was meant to express and ... prepare its students for. What does it profit any of us if we get some hold upon externals but never comprehend the soul of things. This College has a great soul. An idea was worked into its brick and mortar. An ideal hovers perpetually over it. You must have a sense of the cooperation, the fellowship it expresses and the love of learning for learnings' sake, else you will never be fitted to receive its A.B.

Georgia Kendrick
(Lady Principal, 1891-1913)

Vassar Lake, 1873

Town House (Student Residences)

Alumnae House

Alumnae House

Alumnae House

Dear Miriam,

When I thought about our fortieth reunion in June, which I did with surprising intensity for an ancient crone with no particular class spirit, one of its brightest possibilities was that you might be there. I was really cast down when I learned that you would not appear....I hope that we can both totter back to our fiftieth.

Albertina Pitkin Jerome's letter to the class will tell you what we did and saw and heard during the three days at Vassar. I am always impressed when I am there by the union of the past and the future, which produces a sound and vigorous present. And I feel that the College is indeed built upon a rock.

From Rebecca Lowrie to Miriam Ash

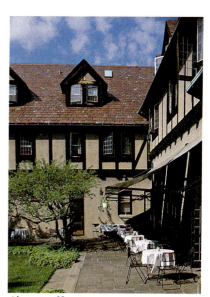

Alumnae House

Taylor Hall

Taylor Gate

Taylor Hall

Vassar
Oct. 9, 1865

My dearest Mother,

. . . I wish you could see old
Mr. Vassar, his face is a perfect
sunbeam, he seems entirely
happy and contented to walk over
the buildings and nod at all the
girls. Every pleasant day his
carriage is here.

From Martha Warner,
Class of 1868

Acknowledgments and Credits

All color photographs by Mark C. Borton and Tyson R. Henry. Historical research by Bonnie Jean Bastow.

We gratefully acknowledge the assistance of Lisa M. Browar and Nancy S. MacKechnie of the Francis Fitz Randolph Rare Book Room of the Lockwood Library.

All original manuscripts, documents, and black-and-white photographs are courtesy of the Francis Fitz Randolph Rare Book Room of the Lockwood Library.

Black-and-white photographs that can be identified by photographer: Page 16, Rollie Thorne McKenna; p. 18, Vail Brothers; pp. 34, 35, Brown Brothers; p. 65, Margaret DeM. Brown; p. 68, Edmund L. Wolven; p. 72, C. Gullman; p. 73, C. B. Borland; p. 75, (top) Vail Brothers, (bottom) Steenson & Van Vlack; p. 79, IBM; p. 84 Rollie Thorne McKenna.

Typesetting, color separations, and printing by The Waverly Printing Company of Portland, Connecticut.

Binding by New Hampshire Bindery, Inc. of Concord, New Hampshire.

Book design by Tom Goddard

Cover design by Kristina Jorgensen Jones